Roman Soldier

Baby

In-line Skates

Mechanic

Astronaut

School Girl

King

Queen

Doctor

African Musician

Mum   Dad

Brother

Sister

Gran   Grandad

Pharaoh

Clown

Skateboarder   Greek Scholar

Cowboy

Flamenco Dancer

Toddler

Judge

Greek Soldier   # Victorian Lady

Rock 'n' Roll Star   Teacher

Black Belt

Sailor

Tennis Player

Builder

Bride　　　　Father Christmas

Roman Emperor   Nurse

opera Singer

Sheriff

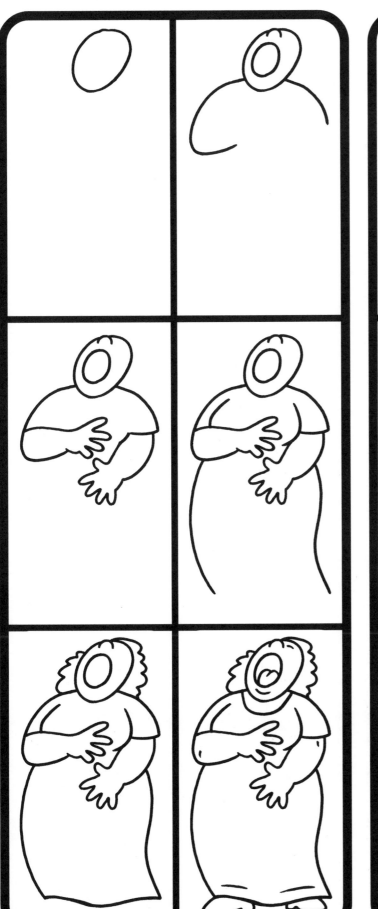

Artist

Witch

Dentist

Soccer Player

Ice Skater

Superhero

Diver

Burglar

Chef

Elf

Cave Woman   # Cave Man

Gardener

Baseball Player

Fairy   Baker

Tightrope Walker   Fisherman

Magician   Knight

Policeman   BMX

Rock'n'Roll Dancer

Postman

Inuit

Scuba Diver

Fireman   Arab

Hippy

Lumberjack

Emperor　　Indian Dancer

Victorian Gentleman

Ballet Dancer

Painter

Farmer

Viking   Jump

Skip

1970s Pop Star

Actor

Handstand

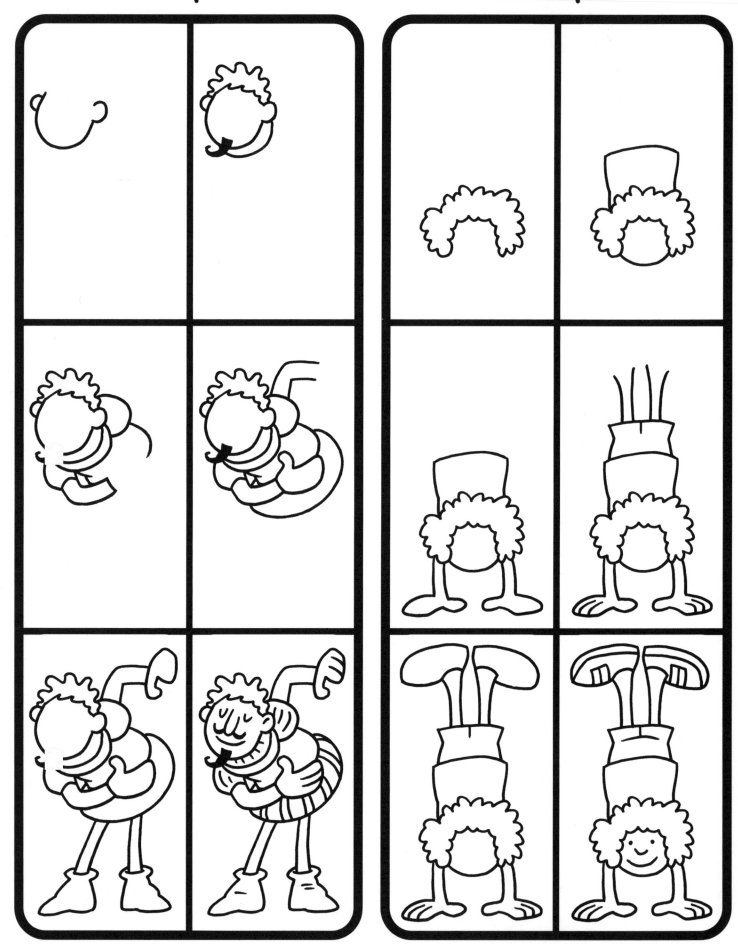

Surgeon

Chinese Lady

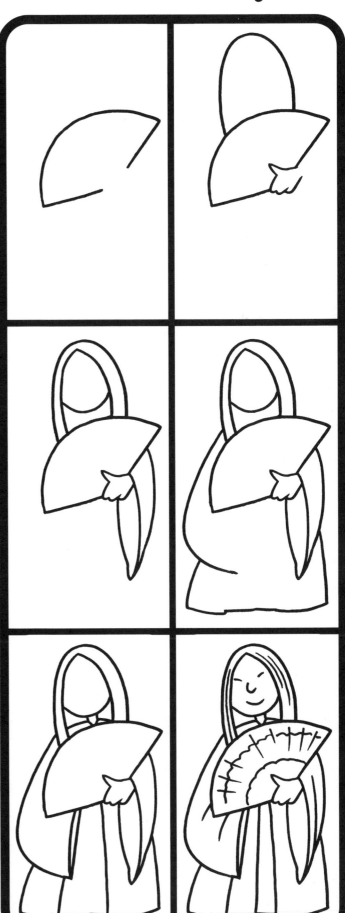

Scientist   Butcher

Pirate

Mountaineer

Deep Sea Diver

Wizard

Captain

Dwarf

Tarzan

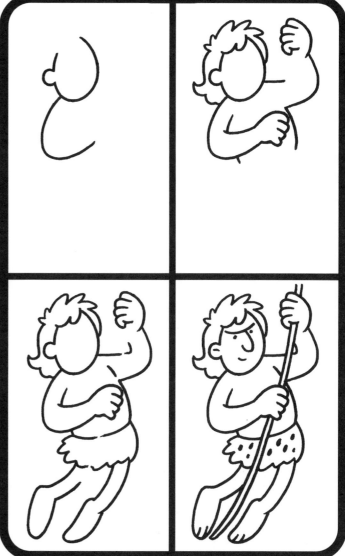

Skier

Surfer

Reverend

High Jumper

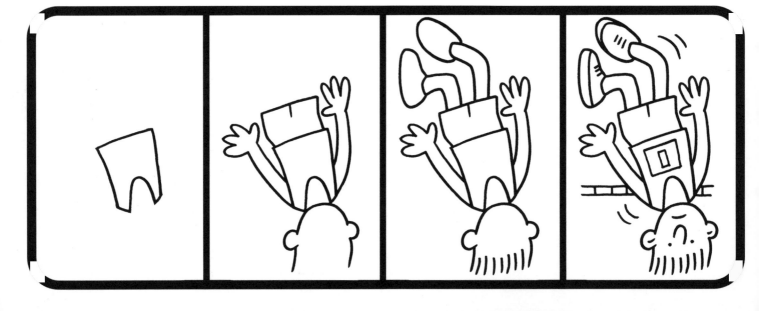

Weightlifter

Juggler

conductor

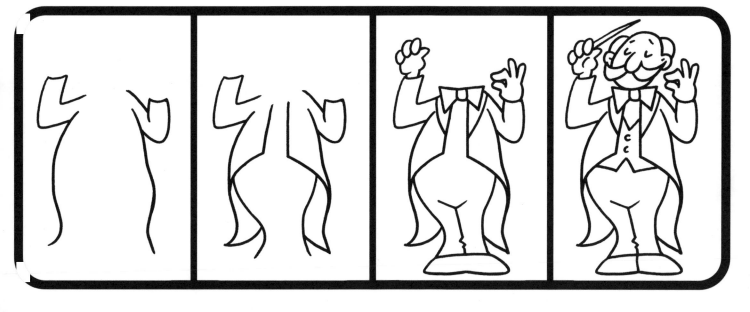

Basketball Player

Waiter

Football Player

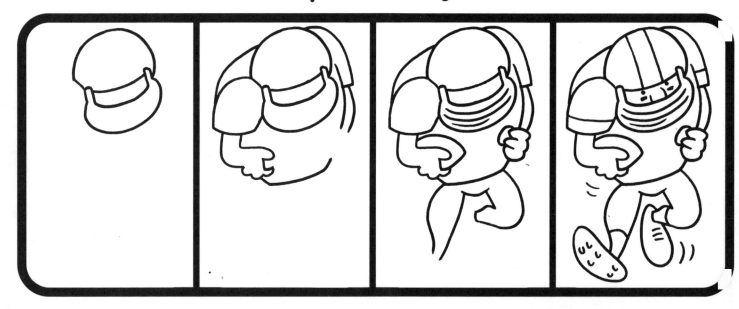